Visual Geography Series®

# NICARAGUA

## ...in Pictures

Prepared by
Nathan A. Haverstock

Lerner Publications Company
Minneapolis

Courtesy of Inter-American Development Bank

**Carlos Alberto Tellez Flores and his sister Rita take a bath with a hose held by their brother Oscar Salvador.**

This book is an all-new edition in the Visual Geography Series. Previous editions were published by Sterling Publishing Company, New York City. The text, set in 10/12 Century Textbook, is fully revised and updated, and new photographs, maps, charts, and captions have been added.

Website address: www.lernerbooks.com

LIBRARY OF CONGRESS CATALOGING-IN-PUBLICATION DATA

Haverstock, Nathan A.
  Nicaragua in pictures.

  (Visual geography series)
  Includes index.
  Summary: Brief text and photographs introduce the geography, history, government, people, and economy of the Central American country largest in area.
   1. Nicaragua. [1. Nicaragua] I. Title. II. Series: Visual geography series (Minneapolis, Minn.)
  F1523.H35   1987   972.85     86–27713
  ISBN 0–8225–1817–1 (lib. bdg.)

International Standard Book Number: 0–8225–1817–1
Library of Congress Catalog Card Number: 86–27713

## VISUAL GEOGRAPHY SERIES®

**Publisher**
Harry Jonas Lerner
**Associate Publisher**
Nancy M. Campbell
**Executive Series Editor**
Mary M. Rodgers
**Assistant Series Editor**
Gretchen Bratvold
**Editorial Assistant**
Nora W. Kniskern
**Illustrations/Editor**
Nathan A. Haverstock
**Consultants/Contributors**
Dr. Ruth F. Hale
Nathan A. Haverstock
Sandra K. Davis
**Designer**
Jim Simondet
**Cartographer**
Carol F. Barrett
**Indexer**
Kristine S. Schubert
**Computer Systems Consultant**
Rhona H. Landsman
**Production Manager**
Gary J. Hansen

Courtesy of Inter-American Development Bank

**These members of a farm cooperative weed onions on lands near the Honduran border.**

**Acknowledgments**

Title page photo courtesy of Inter-American Development Bank.

Elevation contours adapted from *The Times Atlas of the World,* seventh comprehensive edition (New York: Times Books, 1985).

5   6   7   8   9   10   –   I/JR   –   03   02   01   00   99   98

Courtesy of United Nations

Shrimp boats lie at anchor in the Pacific port of San Juan del Sur. The fishing industry in Nicaragua was largely neglected until recent years but is now expanding.

# Contents

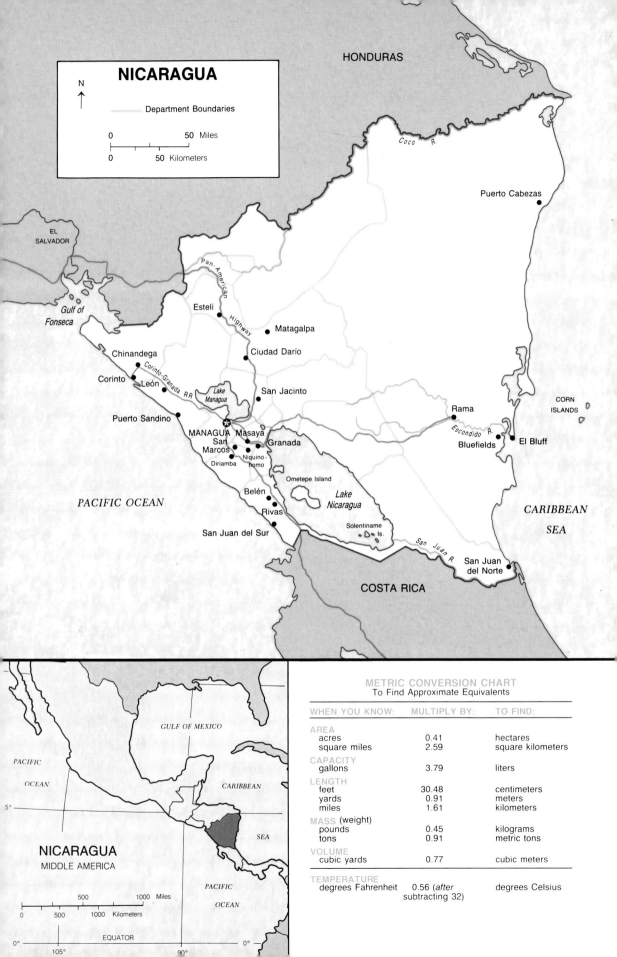

## NICARAGUA

N

Department Boundaries

0           50   Miles

0          50   Kilometers

HONDURAS

Coco R.

Puerto Cabezas

EL SALVADOR

Pan-American Highway

Estelí

Matagalpa

Ciudad Darío

Gulf of Fonseca

Chinandega

Corinto-Granada RR

Corinto

León

Lake Managua

San Jacinto

Puerto Sandino

MANAGUA

Masaya

San Marcos

Granada

Diriamba

Niquinohomo

Rama

Escondido R.

Bluefields

El Bluff

CORN ISLANDS

PACIFIC OCEAN

Belén

Rivas

Ometepe Island

Lake Nicaragua

San Juan del Sur

Solentiname Is.

San Juan R.

San Juan del Norte

CARIBBEAN SEA

COSTA RICA

GULF OF MEXICO

PACIFIC OCEAN

CARIBBEAN SEA

NICARAGUA

MIDDLE AMERICA

PACIFIC OCEAN

5°

105°

90°

0°

0°

EQUATOR

500      1000   Miles

0     500     1000   Kilometers

### METRIC CONVERSION CHART
To Find Approximate Equivalents

| WHEN YOU KNOW: | MULTIPLY BY: | TO FIND: |
| --- | --- | --- |
| **AREA** | | |
| acres | 0.41 | hectares |
| square miles | 2.59 | square kilometers |
| **CAPACITY** | | |
| gallons | 3.79 | liters |
| **LENGTH** | | |
| feet | 30.48 | centimeters |
| yards | 0.91 | meters |
| miles | 1.61 | kilometers |
| **MASS** (weight) | | |
| pounds | 0.45 | kilograms |
| tons | 0.91 | metric tons |
| **VOLUME** | | |
| cubic yards | 0.77 | cubic meters |
| **TEMPERATURE** | | |
| degrees Fahrenheit | 0.56 (*after* subtracting 32) | degrees Celsius |

At a 1985 political rally in the Central Plaza of Managua, the accent is on revolutionary themes. The large red banner *(foreground)* proclaims "The Communist Party of Nicaragua." The message above the portrait of Lenin is "Long live the unity of revolutionary forces." The yellow sign *(center)* lettered in red has the slogan "Shoulder to shoulder, hand to hand, we are brothers – workers and campesinos." In the foreground, a marcher in a red shirt cools his thirst with a Coca-Cola. The white sign *(background right)* calls for "People [and] army united to guarantee the victory" – a reference to the ongoing struggle to defeat U.S.-backed contra rebels. Augusto César Sandino, who was assassinated while resisting the U.S.-backed imposition of the Somoza dictatorship, is the figure in the portrait hanging from the building.

# Introduction

On July 17, 1979, there was jubilation in the streets of Managua. Rebels calling themselves Sandinistas paraded in triumph to celebrate their victory over a father-son dictatorship that had lasted nearly 50 years. Dressed in battle fatigues, the new Sandinista leaders—men and women in their thirties for the most part—were determined to build a new and just society out of the ashes of the troubled past.

Their first task was to care for those who had suffered during the fighting—the orphaned and the homeless of a civil war in which some 30,000 to 50,000 people had been killed and another 100,000 wounded. The global response was generous. During the year following the Sandinista victory, the U.S. Congress voted economic assistance for Nicaragua at the same time that Communist Cuba and the Soviet Union were also providing it.

Unfortunately, all hopes that East-West rivalries might give way to support for Nicaragua's young leaders were soon dashed. Officials of the U.S. Reagan administration grew wary as the Sandinistas welcomed Cuban military advisors, teachers, and socialist institutions. In 1981 the United States cut off aid to Nicaragua, claiming that the Sandinistas were aiding leftist rebels in nearby El Salvador. This made the Sandinistas even more dependent on aid from Soviet-bloc nations.

Nicaraguan business leaders had governed alongside the Sandinistas immediately after the revolution. Some of those who had fought with distinction became disenchanted with the nation's deepening socialism and resigned or went into self-imposed exile. Dissent within the country continued, and the government soon found itself facing armed resistance from a group of opponents called contras. Their operations were funded secretly by the U.S. government and by private citizens who feared that Nicaragua, like Cuba, might become a Communist dictatorship.

**Carlos Enrique Sotelo Sandino was the director of the Eastern Regional Coffee-Growers Cooperative, which was established in 1977 and grew under the Sandinista government to nearly 400 members. The cooperative provided low-cost farm supplies to members and helped them to market their crops.**

The United States conducted huge troop maneuvers along the Honduras-Nicaragua border. Nicaraguan leaders warned their people to expect an invasion by U.S. forces, and the U.S. government warned that Nicaragua was a dangerous Soviet beachhead on the North American mainland. As the political dispute heated up, Nicaragua's economy grew increasingly weak and dependent on aid from the Soviet bloc.

In 1987 the president of neighboring Costa Rica proposed a settlement known as the Guatemala Accord. The treaty established a cease-fire between the Sandinista forces and the contras. It also called for open elections in Nicaragua. Under pressure, the Sandinista leadership signed the accord.

The elections that took place early in 1990 proved to be a turning point for Nicaragua. Daniel Ortega, the Sandinista president of Nicaragua, faced an opposition united behind Violeta Barrios de Chamorro, a prominent and popular newspaper publisher. Although Ortega and the Sandinistas enjoyed a solid base of support, Chamorro emerged as the winner. The Sandinista revolution was over.

In the early 1990s, however, Chamorro's administration ran into trouble. By compromising with the still-powerful Sandinista leaders, the president lost the support of the party that sponsored her in the 1990 elections. By the 1996 election year, the government's plans to improve the nation's economy had faltered, and violence between contras and Sandinistas raged in rural areas. Voters elected Arnoldo Alemán, the conservative former mayor of Managua, to the presidency. Since Alemán took office in early 1997, he has struggled to rebuild the economy by returning land seized by the Sandinistas during the 1980s. The Sandinistas, in turn, have vowed to use violence to stop the redistribution of land. Despite the good intentions of the country's second democratically elected president, Nicaragua faces an uncertain future.

The once-active crater of this volcano has filled with water, forming placid Lake Nejapa.

# 1) The Land

Nicaragua is the largest of the Central American countries. With about 50,000 square miles of territory, it is slightly larger than New York State and slightly smaller than England. To the west, Nicaragua fronts on the Pacific Ocean, while to the east it has a long coastline on the Caribbean Sea.

In the north, rugged mountains cut by silt-laden streams form much of the frontier with Honduras. In the south along the Costa Rican border, Nicaragua is low and swampy. The paved Pan-American Highway in the west is the only well-traveled land route into Honduras in the north and into Costa Rica in the south. The sparsely inhabited and hard-to-patrol border areas proved convenient to anti-Sandinista rebels, and Nicaragua's civil war caused heavy damage in these regions.

## Topography

Nicaragua is situated at the only sizable break in the long chain of mountains that runs along the Pacific coast of the Americas from Alaska to the southern tip of South America. From the Gulf of Fonseca (northwest of Nicaragua), this extensive mountain system takes a sharp turn to the east to disappear under the Caribbean Sea before rising again to form the islands of Cuba, Jamaica, Hispaniola, Puerto Rico, and the smaller islands of the West Indies.

7

Geologically, Nicaragua thus separates North America from the southern portion of Central America, where the mountains rise again to continue their march down the South American continent. For centuries, scientists and entrepreneurs have dreamed of turning this topographical feature to Nicaragua's advantage by building a canal across southern Nicaragua to connect the two oceans.

## Lowlands and Lakes

According to geologists, the lowlands near Nicaragua's lakes are of comparatively recent origin. The evidence for this fact is that both Lake Nicaragua, which measures 100 miles long and 45 miles wide, and the San Juan River that flows out of it have saltwater sea life—including dangerous sharks that have adapted to fresh water. Lake Nicaragua and Lake Mana-

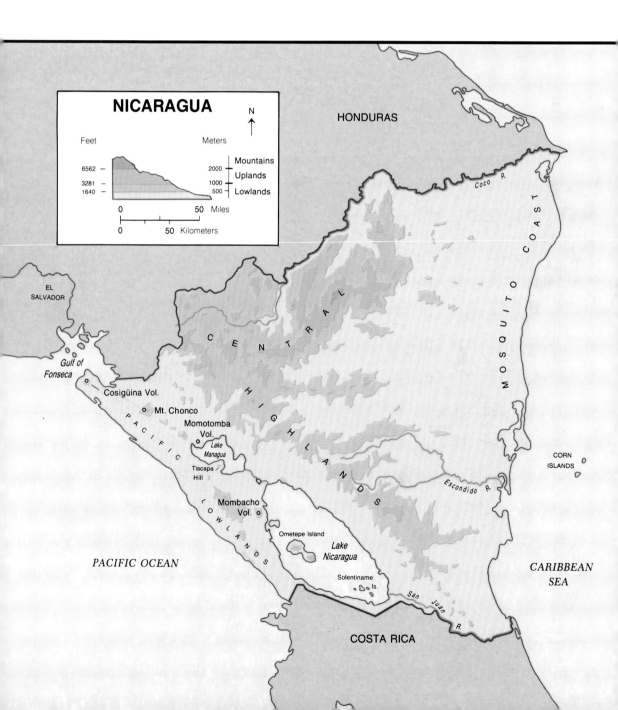

Independent Picture Service

Mount Chonco is one of more than 20 volcanoes that rise up dramatically from the Nicaraguan lowlands.

gua, a 38-mile-long body of water that drains into Lake Nicaragua from the northwest, were probably both once part of the Pacific Ocean. In later prehistoric times, the area of the present-day lakes was encircled by rising land and was raised along with its new surroundings, until it reached an elevation of more than 100 feet above sea level.

## Volcanoes and Earthquakes

Nicaragua's location on a geological rift makes it an area of intense volcanic activity. Mount Cosigüina, which overlooks the Gulf of Fonseca, was formed a century and a half ago in a convulsive explosion that sent clouds of ash as far east as the island of Jamaica.

South of Cosigüina lies a row of more than 20 volcanoes, some of them still active and smoldering. Among the quieter volcanoes of this chain is Momotombo, whose beautifully shaped cone overlooks Lake Nicaragua from the northwest. Within Lake Nicaragua, two volcanoes rise up on Ometepe, the largest island in the

lake. The most continually active volcano is located in the Masaya National Park, just west of Granada—the nation's second most important city.

Earthquakes, too, pose a constant threat to Nicaragua's population centers, most of which are located in the northwest, from the Gulf of Fonseca to Lake Managua. This area lies just west of the volcanic zone and along a rift where the earth's surface is fragile and shifting. The capital city of Managua was shattered by earthquake and fire in 1931, and it is still recovering from an earthquake in 1972 that destroyed most of its central business district.

## Pacific Region

Most Nicaraguans live on a strip of lowlands about 40 miles wide that extends along the Pacific coast from Honduras to Costa Rica. These mostly rolling lowlands, which seldom rise higher than 3,000 feet above sea level, are interrupted in the north by a line of volcanoes and in the south by highlands. The bulk of what Nicaragua produces from the land comes from this rich, breadbasket area—including rice, corn, beans, bananas, cattle, and dairy products. The harvests of this area are

Courtesy of Inter-American Development Bank

These fine brahma cattle, with the characteristic hump, are well adapted to the tropics of Nicaragua.

9

marketed via a well-developed network of roads to such major cities of the region as Managua, Granada, and Chinandega.

## Central Highlands

Farms, most of which are small and produce the staples of life, are numerous in the central highlands as well. The rolling highland terrain lies 2,000 to 5,000 feet above sea level, with the highest peak reaching an elevation of 8,000 feet. Between the forest-covered ridgelines, farming settlements and towns dot valleys that point like long fingers toward the Caribbean Sea.

## Caribbean Lowlands

Hot, humid tropical lowlands in the east constitute nearly one-third of Nicaragua's national territory. These lowlands—named the Mosquito Coast after the disease-carrying insect that once spread fever among the inhabitants—extend along the Caribbean in a band nearly 100 miles wide in the north near the Honduran border and about 50 miles wide in the south on the Costa Rican frontier.

Unlike the productive lowlands along the Pacific, the Caribbean lowlands are sparsely inhabited, swampy, and unhealthful places to live. There are no all-weather land routes from populous western Nicaragua to most settlements along the Caribbean. In central Nicaragua, for example, people and commerce travel by paved highway as far as the town of Rama, where the journey must be continued via the Escondido River to the important Caribbean port of Bluefields. In the north another port, Puerto Cabezas, is served by roads that can be used only during dry weather.

Nicaragua's Caribbean lowlands—with mangrove islands, sluggish and brackish rivers, and inhospitable swamps—resemble sparsely inhabited areas of Florida and Louisiana. Two major rivers help drain

**Hilly land is used to produce crops such as maize (corn) and other vegetables.**

substantial areas of Nicaragua's lowlands. The Coco River—Central America's longest—forms more than half the border with Honduras to the north before emptying into the Caribbean. The San Juan River in the south forms much of the border with Costa Rica. Several other rivers, including the Escondido, provide needed drainage in areas of heavy rainfall.

Nicaragua owns several small islands offshore in the Caribbean. The best known are the Corn Islands. Popular vacation resorts today, they were formerly leased to the United States for use as part of an international air traffic control system.

## Climate

The climate of Nicaragua is heavily influenced by warm winds that blow inland from both coasts. Major areas of settlement are typically tropical—hot and humid at noon, warm in the morning and afternoon, and pleasant at night. As in other tropical areas, altitude moderates both heat and humidity. The highland areas of northwest Nicaragua are noticeably cooler than the rest of the nation, with mean average temperatures of 60° to 70° F, compared to 80° F in much of the rest of the nation.

Rainfall varies substantially. The Pacific region sees about 60 inches per year, and the central highlands receive up to 100 inches. Rainfall in the Caribbean lowlands ranges from 165 inches annually in the north to 250 inches in the south, making this region the rainiest in Central America.

## Flora and Fauna

In view of Nicaragua's heavy rainfall, it is not surprising that rain-forests cover much of the lowlands. Great trees standing more than 100 feet in height—with trunks that are four to five feet in diameter—are common. They raise skyward a leafy canopy, beneath which there is a profusion of wildlife. Mammals include jaguars, pumas, monkeys, armadillos, anteaters, and peccaries. Crocodiles lurk in lowland waters, and the swamps abound with turtles. Snakes are numerous. Long boa constrictors wait concealed in the murky water for their prey, and poisonous serpents, including coral snakes and pit vipers, thrive in the Caribbean lowlands.

Independent Picture Service

Central America and the West Indies host a richly profuse bird population.

Extensive grasslands, with scattered stands of pine, lie among swampier areas of the coast. Along the Caribbean seashore itself, which has few good beaches, are forests of coconut palms, and the sea is home to a rich array of fish.

In the central highlands, sizable forests yield commercially valuable hardwoods, including mahogany. The highland valleys

Mahogany logs float down the Escondido River. Mahogany has been a valuable Nicaraguan export since the eighteenth century.

Independent Picture Service

11

Photo by David Mangurian

This malinche tree in Belén, near the Costa Rican border, is in full bloom. The tree takes its name from an Aztec Indian woman who served as interpreter to the Spanish conquistador Hernán Cortés during the conquest of Mexico.

and slopes that face away from the rain-laden east winds are semi-arid and covered with scrub brush and soils of little value.

Nicaragua's birdlife is extraordinarily varied, with winged visitors from both North and South America. Chicadees, waxwings, titmice, swallows, flycatchers, warblers, thrushes, mockingbirds, wrens, orioles, blackbirds, and jays compete for territory with bright-plumed parrots and macaws. Quail and ducks are found in the countryside, where hawks, ospreys, and falcons prey on smaller birds and rodents. The scavenging buzzard is common throughout Nicaragua. Along the seashore, large wading birds—including herons and ibis—preen their feathers, while grebes, gulls, terns, pelicans, and cormorants patrol overhead on the lookout for something to eat in the water down below.

## Managua

Managua, the largest city (population 682,000), is the capital and chief commercial center of Nicaragua. A spread-out place, the city lacks a well-defined downtown. The central business district was leveled in 1972 by an earthquake. Central

Managua became an eerie wasteland of empty fields, dominated by a few concrete or stone buildings that survived the shock. These structures include the Palace of the Heroes of the Revolution (formerly the National Palace), the Presidential Palace, a sports stadium, and the cathedral—the lat-

Courtesy of Inter-American Development Bank

The skyline of Managua is seen against the backdrop of Lake Managua.

ter, though damaged, still stands and is being restored.

Meanwhile, new business and residential areas were built on the outskirts of the city in order to accommodate the rapidly expanding urban population. Over time these areas took on a life of their own, so that Managua has become a collection of suburbs, each with its own social and economic structure.

The city stands on the Pan-American Highway, Nicaragua's only major roadway, which runs across the nation from Honduras to Costa Rica. A network of secondary roads links the capital with most other economically important parts of the country. Overlooking the city is the hill of Tiscapa, on which stand the solidly built forts and palaces that house the nation's rulers. According to a proverb that has proven true in this century, whoever holds Tiscapa is master of Nicaragua.

Managua was founded in the 1850s on the site of an Indian community. The city's

The cathedral of León, the largest in Central America, was begun in 1746 and took over a century to build. Inside are several religious treasures, including a famous shrine — the gift of Spain's King Philip II.

location represented a compromise between Nicaragua's two chief political parties, the Liberals and the Conservatives. Previously, the capital had alternated between León, stronghold of the Liberals, and Granada, bastion of the Conservatives. Managua was located halfway between the two, on the southern shore of Lake Managua.

## Secondary Cities

León (population 85,000) was founded in 1524 at the foot of Momotombo Volcano, which overlooks Lake Managua. When an earthquake destroyed León in 1609, the city was moved to its present site some 30 miles northwest of Managua. León has a long and proud history, and it is still considered the intellectual capital of the nation. Its university, around which the life of the city revolves, was founded in 1804. The city has an ancient air, with carefully preserved, narrow streets of low adobe homes with red-tiled roofs. It boasts Central America's largest cathedral, whose

The swimming pool at Managua's Intercontinental Hotel is viewed from a hotel room. The Intercontinental is favored by foreign visitors. After the 1979 revolution, guests from the Soviet bloc and journalists of many nationalities stayed in its comfortable quarters.

During the 1972 earthquake entire blocks of buildings in Managua were flattened.

cornerstone was laid in 1746 and whose construction took a century. The people of León were strong supporters of Nicaragua's recent revolution. During 1978 and 1979, the city was the scene of heavy fighting, and the damage has yet to be repaired.

Granada (population 60,000) also dates its founding to 1524, though its location at the foot of another volcano, Mombacho, on the shores of Lake Nicaragua, has remained unchanged. Located at the end of the railway from the Pacific port of Corinto, Granada is a wealthy trading center and the commercial hub of a region of productive farms and cattle ranches. Like León, Granada is well endowed with colonial architecture, including a Franciscan church said to date from 1523.

Granada's wealthy merchant class, the bulwark of conservatism in Nicaragua, has survived many ups and downs. Gravestones in the old cemetery record deaths during pirate attacks in the seventeenth century and during the invasion by William Walker in 1857. The city of Granada, like Masaya some five miles to the west, was the scene of much fighting during Nicaragua's 1979 revolution.

Masaya (population 50,000) is the center of a prosperous agricultural region. With railway service to the coast, Masaya is the place where many of Nicaragua's commodity exports—including tobacco, coffee, cotton, cacao, and sugar—are traded before entering world commerce. The large public market near the railway station is famous

The Pan-American Highway spans a stream in western Nicaragua.

for shops that offer the country's finest handicrafts.

Chinandega (population 50,000) is located inland, on the Pan-American Highway about midway between León and the Honduran border. Its importance rests on its trade in Nicaraguan cotton and grain. Among other crops grown in the area are coffee and sugarcane. Cattle are also raised.

Farther inland and about 50 miles north of Managua stand two towns of strategic importance, Matagalpa (population 30,000) and Estelí (25,000). Located in somewhat rugged areas, these towns figured importantly in the revolution. For rebel troops descending from the mountains of northern Nicaragua, Matagalpa and Estelí were primary objectives. By controlling them, rebels could threaten Managua and position themselves for military raids to choke off the commercial lifelines leading to Nicaragua.

Courtesy of Inter-American Development Bank

**Much destruction occurred during the street fighting of the 1979 revolution. Whole blocks, such as this one in Estelí, were demolished.**

**Young, well-armed Sandinista troops were a common sight in post-revolutionary Nicaragua. These soldiers in Estelí guarded a war-damaged building used by officials of the Sandinista government.**

Courtesy of Latin American Service

**15**

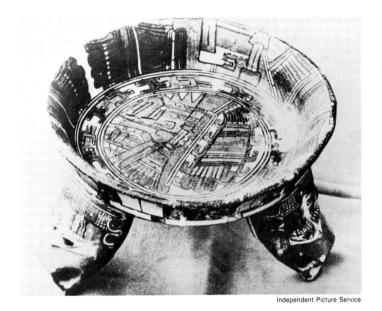

# 2) History and Government

Like the rest of Central America, Nicaragua was a mixing bowl of Indian cultures before the arrival of the Spaniards. In pre-Columbian times, seafaring Indians from Mexico and from the Andean nations of South America may have traded up and down the Nicaraguan coast. During the course of many centuries, Indians from the area now known as Nicaragua developed regular overland contacts between people to the north and south.

## Pre-Columbian Indians

Anthropologists have identified three early cultures in Nicaragua. The Pacific lowlands and western highlands were set-tled by Indians apparently related to the Indians of Mexico. The Pipils, a Nahua-speaking tribe from Mexico, drifted (or were driven) during several centuries into El Salvador and Nicaragua. They developed a culture similar in some respects to those of the Maya and Aztecs of Guatemala and Mexico. They worshipped some of the same gods, had a similar calendar for determining the seasons, and used a system of counting like that of the Maya. Carvings of a plumed serpent, a Mexican Indian symbol, were made in Nicaragua in pre-Columbian times. Pottery styles and decorative motifs on buildings all bore a close relation to those common among Mexican Indians.

Elaborately worked ceramics have been found throughout the Pacific lowlands of Nicaragua. Indians of the extinct Mangue-Chorotega culture used this vessel for storing incense. This and other Indian artifacts may be seen at the museum in Nindirí, near Masaya.

A second culture existed in the southeastern lowlands of Nicaragua and on portions of the Mosquito Coast. Here, a language related to that of the Chibcha Indians of Colombia was (and still is) spoken. Just north of San Juan del Norte in Nicaragua, archaeologists recently made an important find—the remains of an ancient city that had had a population of some 100,000 people. Excavations indicate that the people who inhabited the city were somewhat similar to those of northern South America. Some archaeologists believe that the city bears similarities to those of the Incas of Peru. The drinking of chicha, a fermented corn liquor widely consumed in northern and western South America, is another sign of a possible early Nicaraguan relationship with that area.

A third culture native to Nicaragua appears to have flourished along the Mosquito Coast—a culture related to the civilizations of such Caribbean island groups as the Arawaks. In Nicaragua, these peoples made common use of *bohíos* —round thatched huts also widely used among Caribbean peoples. The use of the word *canoa* (an Arawak term that refers to many different styles of boats) also indicates some kinship between the Nicaraguan and Caribbean Indian cultures.

This *metate* (a stone used for grinding corn) has the shape of a jaguar — a sacred symbol to the Maya and Olmecs — suggesting the Mexican Indian influences in Nicaragua.

## Spanish Conquest

The Spanish conquest of present-day Nicaragua was carried out independently from two directions. From the southeast, Pedro Arias Dávila, the governor of Panama, sent out an expedition in 1522 to find out what lay to the north and west of the Isthmus of Panama. The members of the expedition encountered some fairly advanced Indians, relatives of the Maya of Mexico, and returned to Panama with an impressive store of gold ornaments. From the northwest, Hernán Cortés, the conqueror of Mexico, sent one of his lieutenants, Pedro de Alvarado, to claim the area.

By 1530 Alvarado had brought much of Central America under his control.

From Panama, Arias vainly protested Alvarado's intrusion into what he considered his territory. The Spaniards from Mexico, backed by the greater power and wealth of New Spain (as Mexico was then known), won out. The Spanish crown confirmed Alvarado as governor of Guatemala in 1525 and placed the territory of Nicaragua within his jurisdiction. Because boundaries of the area were vague, however, Arias continued to insist that he was governor of Nicaragua, even though he was not actually in control of the area.

Courtesy of Museum of Modern Art of Latin America

Plays about the conquest period, in which Indians lose militarily but triumph spiritually, have been revived in Niquinohomo, a village near Masaya. Rehearsals take place in this church from the colonial era.

Displaying a skull-and-crossbones flag as a warning of danger to life, pirates board a Spanish vessel by moonlight.

In the meantime, Alvarado, a vigorous leader, opened up a transportation route from Granada—the principal settlement on the northwestern shore of Lake Nicaragua—to the Caribbean Sea via Lake Nicaragua and the San Juan River. Alvarado's forces also fortified the mouth of the river and the adjoining lowland areas. With the opening of a sea-to-sea transportation route and Alvarado's consolidation of his power in the area, the conquest period of Nicaragua's history came to a close.

## Colonial Period

Three centuries of Spanish rule brought to Nicaragua the Roman Catholic faith, the Spanish language and culture, and a system of government familiar to Spanish colonies everywhere in the New World. With its comparatively limited resources of land and precious minerals, Nicaragua did not attract as many settlers as Mexico or Peru and was largely neglected by the Spanish crown.

### SETTLERS

The Spanish established their Nicaraguan seat of government at León. During the three centuries of colonial history, Nicaragua enjoyed a high degree of local self-government and only rarely was subject to the attention of the captain general in Guatemala City. Priests came to settle with the Spanish conquerors, and the first Roman Catholic church was established at Granada in 1524. Catholicism, bolstered by the influence of schools run by priests, took deep root among the inhabitants of the area.

The Spanish settlers lived mostly along the Pacific on farms and ranches. They used Indians or imported black slaves to produce cacao for export and cattle and food for local consumption. The Spaniards made few inroads through Nicaragua's Caribbean coastal lowlands, which remained largely the haunt of buccaneers—French, Dutch, and British pirates whose numbers were increased by runaway slaves from various parts of the Caribbean.

### PIRATES

Pirates frequently raided the towns of Nicaragua. Their marauding was helped by the ease with which oceangoing vessels could travel up the San Juan River. After the point at which large ships could go no farther, smaller boats could reach and cross Lake Nicaragua. At Granada, on the lakeshore, the pirates plundered stores of gold and indigo and carried their spoils off to Europe. The pirates also benefited from Spain's casual attitude toward the value of Nicaragua's potential booty. Nicaragua was not rich enough, the Spanish believed, to merit its own fortifications. Instead, powerful forts at Veracruz (on Mexico's Caribbean coast) and at Portobelo (in Panama) were relied upon to stop would-be pillagers. So free and easy was the business of looting in poorly defended Nicaragua that a Dutch buccaneer, Abraham Blauvelt, was able to found the settlement of Bluefields in 1633. The new town helped establish what enduring contacts there were between outsiders and the local Rama and Sumu Indians.

Only in 1672 did Spain bother to fortify the mouth of the San Juan River. By then treaties with Great Britain—under which Spain yielded its claim to exclusive rights of settlement in the New World—had reduced the need for defense. The treaties provided Great Britain with a foothold in the area and the right to trade in slaves and various commodities.

The heavy, square rigging of this ship was typical of the galleon—a sailing ship used for war or commerce by the Spanish from the fifteenth to the early eighteenth centuries.

## The Eighteenth Century

Economic progress in Nicaragua was uneven. There were spurts of activity after 1741—encouraged by one of Nicaragua's few progressive colonial administrators—and after 1778. When Spain sided against Great Britain during the U.S. War of Independence, Archibald Campbell, the governor of Jamaica—which was then a British colony—sent a hostile expedition to Nicaragua. He intended to cut the Spanish Empire in two and open a canal route to the Pacific, but the expedition came to nothing. The British continued trying to stir up revolt in Nicaragua by making the Miskito chiefs their allies. Eventually, however, Great Britain agreed to evacuate its subjects from the area of the Mosquito Coast in 1786.

Later in the eighteenth century, a new race of people settled in Nicaragua's coastal lowlands. The black Caribs were of mixed black-and-Indian bloodlines. Their ancestors were the fierce Carib tribe of the West Indies. Deported as troublemakers from their British-controlled island homes, the black Caribs were deposited on the Bay Islands off Honduras's coast, from which they spread into nearby areas of Nicaragua.

By the end of the eighteenth century, Nicaragua was home to about 180,000 people, most of whom were mestizos (people of mixed Indian-and-Spanish bloodlines) who lived along the Pacific coast. By then León had become a graceful colonial city that, though subordinate to Guatemala City, had assumed importance as the focus of political, administrative, cultural, and religious life in the colony.

## Independence

Though a neglected region of Spain's New World empire, Nicaragua was not entirely untouched by the new ideas that were sweeping through the Western world during the eighteenth century. Like other groups throughout the Americas, some Nicaraguans were deeply impressed by the success of both the French and North American revolutions and cherished the thought of becoming independent themselves.

In 1811 the town of Rivas in southern Nicaragua boldly declared its independence from Spain and elected a provisional government consisting of Creoles, or Nicaraguan-born inhabitants. Some 5,000 people, including some from the surrounding area, supported the move—mostly because independence would free them from the burdensome taxes imposed by Spain. Spanish troops from nearby Costa Rica quickly ended the revolt, but the uprising, one of the earliest in the Viceroyalty of New Spain, was not in vain. Before the year was out, a similar rebellion broke out to the north in Granada. The rebels sought major reforms in Spanish rule, and, if possible, even independence.

The sentiments of the people of Rivas eventually took root throughout Central America. On September 15, 1821, all of the areas within the captaincy general of Guatemala jointly declared their independence from Spain.

## Federation of Central America

During the next two decades, several attempts were made to forge a Central American union. In the year following their declaration of independence, Central American leaders accepted an invitation from Agustín de Iturbide to join the Mexican Empire, of which he had declared himself the leader. Mexico, however, soon sent its troops to Nicaragua, El Salvador, and Honduras. Liberals in these areas were bitterly opposed to trading their newly found freedom for Mexican domination and resisted.

By the time order was restored, Iturbide had resigned. In 1823 a congress in Guatemala City declared an end to the association with Mexico and established the Federation of Central America. By the time the first National Congress of the new union met in 1825, Nicaragua and other Central American nations were fearful that Guatemala would dominate the federation.

Within Nicaragua, political differences over the Central American union led to conflict. Conservatives, who wanted a strong central government, and Liberals, who wanted a weak one, fought against each other in a civil war that lasted for three years, from 1826 to 1829. Two outstanding leaders, José Cecilio del Valle of Costa Rica and Francisco Morazán of Honduras—who is still honored throughout Central America—attempted to bridge these two poles of opinion through compromise.

Eventually, however, the disagreement had so weakened the federation that Morazán sought to hold it together by force—a tactic that led to revolt. The leader of the uprising was Guatemalan Rafael Carrera, who, with Conservative backing, ousted Morazán. Carrera's victory broke up the federation in 1842 and set off a bloodbath —the massacre of Liberals everywhere in Central America, including Nicaragua.

In 1842 El Salvador, Honduras, and Nicaragua formed a new federation without Guatemala. This new union lasted for just two years before Nicaragua found itself under attack by its two confederates. Thus began a pattern of political infighting still evident in Central America—a pattern whereby people of similar political views conspire with one another across borders to protect or expand their influence.

Independent Picture Service

This bronze equestrian statue honors Francisco Morazán, a Honduran. A leader of the Liberal faction in Central American politics during the strife that followed the end of Spanish rule, Morazán was the last president of the ill-fated Federation of Central America.

ing transportation for 20,000 U.S. citizens per month via Nicaragua. Soon thereafter, Vanderbilt was supporting the goals of William Walker, a U.S. adventurer who wanted to take control of Nicaragua.

## William Walker

A native of Nashville, Tennessee, William Walker made a name for himself as a soldier of fortune and an imperialist. The U.S. poet Joaquin Miller, who served with Walker briefly, described him as a man with "a piercing eye, a princely air, a presence like a chevalier." Walker's career, however, hardly justified such an ennobling description.

In 1853 Walker led an unsuccessful expedition to take over Mexico's territories of Lower California and Sonora. Encouraged by a San Francisco financier named Byron Cole, Walker became interested in Nicaragua as the keystone of a fancied

## Nationhood

Political instability and repeated interference in Nicaraguan affairs by Rafael Carrera (who went on to become dictator of Guatemala) made Nicaragua's first years as a nation stormy ones. By 1850 its population was static at about 250,000. So many male Nicaraguans had been killed in various Central American wars that women outnumbered men in some places by as much as five to one.

Not until the discovery of gold in California in 1848 did Nicaragua receive an economic shot in the arm. Thousands of hopeful prospectors from the United States made their way across Nicaragua en route to the gold diggings. This southern route was safer and quicker than crossing the continental United States. By 1852 the Accessory Transit Company of U.S. tycoon Cornelius Vanderbilt was provid-

Independent Picture Service

The U.S. poet Joaquin Miller served with William Walker and admired his "princely air."

22

Caribbean Federation—to be allied with the southern United States.

Walker was backed by some powerful people from the United States, who wanted to see Nicaragua annexed to the United States as a slave state. In 1855 Walker and 58 adventurers captured the town of Rivas and soon had control of the entire country. He set up a government headed by himself and—aided by a small group of loyal followers—proceeded to impose his rule on the country. Though Nicaraguans resented Walker, Liberals tried to use him against their Conservative foes. Then, after a falling out with Walker, Vanderbilt began supporting Nicaraguan Conservatives to undermine Walker.

The turning point of Walker's fortunes came on September 14, 1856, when his 300 men were completely defeated by half that many Nicaraguans in the Battle of San Jacinto. Though hardly more than a skirmish, it was the first time Walker's men had been defeated, and it destroyed the myth of his unconquerable strength.

From that day on, Walker moved closer

Independent Picture Service

Cornelius "Commodore" Vanderbilt was a U.S. railway and transportation tycoon who attempted to take over Nicaragua through William Walker.

and closer to ultimate defeat, which occurred, ironically, at Rivas in 1857. Walker surrendered there to a U.S. naval officer, went to New Orleans (where he received a hero's welcome), and soon returned to Central America—where he was captured and shot dead.

## The Late Nineteenth Century

A period of reconstruction followed the National War, as the struggle against Walker is known in Nicaragua. In 1858 a new constitution was adopted and Managua became the capital of Nicaragua—a compromise between the Liberals of León and the Conservatives of Granada. The first president elected under the new constitution, Tomás Martínez, governed wisely for eight years, from 1859 to 1867.

Martínez was followed by eight presidents—all but one served four-year terms. Some development and modernization took place during this period. Telegraph service began in 1876, and a submarine

Independent Picture Service

William Walker, a military adventurer from the United States, tried unsuccessfully to take over Nicaragua in the 1850s.

cable linked Nicaragua to the outside world in 1882. There was diplomatic success, too. Under the 1880 Treaty of Managua, Great Britain ceded to Nicaragua all of its claims to the Mosquito Coast, although the local government there continued to function independently for another 14 years.

For three decades, from 1863 to 1893, the Conservative party provided Nicaragua with more or less stable rule, naming presidents and quelling uprisings. Coffee production was expanded and bananas were introduced. Europeans immigrated to Nicaragua and became landowners, introducing new farming methods. This era of tranquillity came to an end in 1895, when a Liberal, José Santos Zelaya, took power by force and subjected the country to 16 years of tyranny.

Zelaya's rule brought material progress —railways were extended, new steamers plied the lakes, public schools were established, and coffee production increased— but the price of progress was high. Graft and corruption enriched Zelaya and his supporters, while conservative opponents were brutally persecuted and harassed. Even Liberal colleagues were betrayed. Liberty vanished, and critics—lucky if they could escape jail, torture, or assassination—fled into self-imposed exile.

When Zelaya was unsuccessful at promoting a new Central American union under his leadership, he stirred up repeated revolts in nearby countries. Zelaya's activities disturbed the region so much that Mexico and the United States convened a peace conference, held in Washington, D.C., in 1907. The conference led to the formation of the Central American Court to settle regional disputes. All, the participants in the conference also signed a pledge to forego stirring up revolutions in nearby territories. Zelaya signed, too, but he did not change his ways.

To maintain order, the United States landed marines at Bluefields on the Caribbean coast in 1909. Zelaya, without friends at home or abroad, fled into exile, leaving his country in a state of disorder. Nicaraguans turned to Washington, D.C., for help, and thus began an era of U.S. intervention.

## The United States Intervenes

The United States sent Thomas C. Dawson to Managua to prepare a Nicaraguan version of the reorganization plan he had drawn up earlier when the United States intervened in the Dominican Republic. Under Dawson's scheme, the rival political factions would agree on a single candidate for president, and Nicaragua would accept a U.S. collector of customs. This customs official would exercise enormous power in Nicaragua, dividing revenues among the Nicaraguan government and foreign creditors. When the nation's debts to the United States were paid off, New York bankers would provide a loan with which to pay off British creditors—a move that would strengthen U.S. influence in the Caribbean.

Many U.S. senators were opposed to a treaty containing provisions that would, in effect, abridge Nicaraguan sovereignty. President William H. Taft, however, avoided the need for Senate approval by using an executive agreement—a type of accord not subject to Senate ratification— to appoint a U.S. collector of Nicaraguan customs. New York bankers made several small loans to the country. As collateral, they took a controlling interest in the Nicaraguan National Bank and the state-owned railways.

By 1912 Nicaragua's standing as a sovereign republic was in doubt. The nation was in debt to New York bankers, who were acting informally for the U.S. president but without the authorization of the U.S. Senate.

### U.S. MARINES
The out-of-power Liberals revolted against the Conservative choice for Nic-

William Howard Taft, U.S. president from 1909 to 1913, increased U.S. control of Nicaragua without the approval of the U.S. Senate.

aragua's president, and the slogan "Down with Yankee imperialists!" became the Liberal battle cry. When the United States landed the marines again, they ended the revolt and kept the Conservative president, Adolfo Díaz, in office. For 19 of the next 21 years, U.S. Marines remained on Nicaraguan soil. Although the marine unit was small—usually no more than 100 men—the meaning of their presence was clear.

Supporters of U.S. intervention claimed that life and liberty were threatened and had to be protected. They also cited the strategic need to guard the Panama Canal, which was opened in 1914. Many people now, however, see the intervention as a case of dollar diplomacy—the use of guns to protect Wall Street investments in gold mines, plantations, railways, and the Nicaraguan National Bank.

Despite U.S. intervention, Nicaragua remained poor and sparsely populated. Most of the country's 750,000 people were engaged in subsistence farming or in raising coffee and bananas on foreign-owned plantations.

### CANAL RIGHTS

The United States further intervened by forcing Nicaragua into a treaty, which was signed in 1914 and ratified by the U.S. Senate in 1916. The treaty gave the United States a claim to any future canal route by way of the San Juan River, in return for a payment of $3 million. A bargain for the United States, the treaty insured that no foreign power could build a waterway to compete with the U.S.-owned Panama Canal—but it raised a furor in Central America. Costa Rica protested that Nicaragua could not give up San Juan River rights, since the river was shared as a boundary by both countries. El Salvador objected that one provision of the treaty, which granted the United States the right to build a naval base on the Gulf of Fonseca, posed a threat to its national security.

The various disputes were submitted to the Central American Court, whose creation the United States had encouraged. The court decided for the plaintiffs, Costa Rica and El Salvador. But the United States refused to abide by the court's decision and enraged Nicaraguans by insisting —with force on its side—that the $3 million go not solely to the Nicaraguan government but also be apportioned among the country's foreign creditors. Since the United States was Nicaragua's main foreign creditor, it was in effect asking for a payment to itself.

## U.S. Occupation

By 1925, when New York bankers had recovered their loans, U.S. president Calvin Coolidge decided that the marines could be safely withdrawn. The Liberals and Conservatives, however, renewed their civil war as soon as the last marine had departed. While the U.S. minister had enough influence to restore Conservative

**25**

Adolfo Díaz to the presidency, Liberals set up a rival administration on the east coast under Juan B. Sacasa.

On the eve of an apparent defeat of President Díaz in 1927 by the rebel Sacasa, U.S. president Coolidge sent battleships into Nicaraguan waters to land 2,000 marines and deliver arms to Díaz's troops. He also promised financial assistance to the Díaz-controlled Conservative government. On the heels of the marines, President Coolidge sent Henry L. Stimson to persuade all factions to lay down their arms and abide by the outcome of a U.S.-sponsored election. As a precautionary measure, the United States began training a Nicaraguan national guard. Called the Guardia Nacional, this body was intended to serve as the major military force in the country, replacing the local armed forces that had proved better at meddling in politics than at preserving order.

The next year the elections gave the presidency to Liberal José María Mon-

Independent Picture Service

In 1927 President Calvin Coolidge ordered the invasion and occupation of Nicaragua by U.S. forces to maintain the Conservative government.

cada, who ruled—closely watched by the marines—with reasonable success. He was unable, however, to stop the opposition of General Augusto César Sandino, a rebel who refused to accept the political accord and kept up a prolonged revolt with a handful of ill-equipped guerrilla troops. Sandino kept the marines off balance until 1933. During this time he developed tactics and strategies of guerrilla warfare that have since been used to great effect by guerrillas in all parts of the world. The marines responded by developing counterinsurgency tactics—including the first use of air power—that have served well against other guerrilla groups.

Though Sandino finally laid down his arms voluntarily, he was treacherously shot by officers of the Guardia Nacional. The marine occupation ended in 1933, when U.S. president Franklin D. Roosevelt announced the Good Neighbor Policy. The same year, Juan B. Sacasa—the oldtime Liberal whom President Coolidge had so strongly opposed—won Nicaragua's presidential election.

Nevertheless, the highly effective Guardia Nacional, against which no rebel force could hope to stand, became the real ruler of the country. The marines departed, and Nicaragua was at the mercy of the Guardia's astute commander, Anastasio ("Tacho") Somoza García.

## The Somoza Dynasty

For 40 years, two generations of Somozas controlled the previously unstable Nicaraguan republic. The first in the Somoza line, Tacho Somoza, was born in the town of San Marcos in the coffee-producing department (province) of Carazo in 1895. Like the two sons who would rule after him, the elder Somoza was schooled in the United States. He also worked for a time in the automobile business in Philadelphia. These experiences provided him with two assets of great value in his rise to power— the ability to converse colloquially in the

Until recently Nicaragua has been a close ally of the United States. This Nicaraguan artillery unit is practicing military maneuvers during World War II.

English language and an understanding of U.S. politics and culture.

After returning to his homeland, the young Somoza rose within the ranks of the Guardia Nacional. By the time the U.S. Marines had departed, Somoza was in command of the Guardia, the power behind President Sacasa.

Within three years Somoza and Sacasa had a falling out, and Somoza used the power of the Guardia to unseat Sacasa and clear the way for his own election as president in 1937. From then until his assassination in 1956, Tacho Somoza ruled supreme in Nicaragua, with a brief interim from 1947 to 1950 when three of his associates were in and out of office in quick succession.

### TACHO SOMOZA'S RULE

"Nicaragua es mi finca" (Nicaragua is my farm), Somoza was quoted as saying, which was almost literally true. The longer he ruled, the more economic power he and trusted members of his family came to wield in Nicaragua. At the time of his death, his personal fortune was worth between $60 and $300 million. He owned some 10 to 15 percent of all the land under cultivation in Nicaragua.

Tacho delighted in riding about the Nicaraguan countryside in his official blue Cadillac, often stopping to rest at one of his many farms. On these trips, which were popular with the Nicaraguan people, he usually wore a white ten-gallon hat and a holstered revolver. To add to the show, he was often accompanied by an impressive parade of vehicles carrying his palace guards. On some occasions, aircraft patrolled the skies over the route of Somoza's caravan.

Though greedy, Tacho Somoza was not generally considered a cruel man. Yet,

his enemies wisely sought the safety of New York City or some other foreign destination before denouncing him. At home and abroad, Somoza was given to praising democracy, but he also felt that Nicaraguans were not ready for the full exercise of democracy. He saw himself as a benevolent leader preparing his fellow citizens gradually for democracy. Somoza's foreign policy was firmly anti-Communist and pro-United States.

### SOMOZA'S ACHIEVEMENTS

Tacho Somoza was a builder. He is credited with having built schools and hospitals throughout the country. Outsiders often expressed genuine enthusiasm about the success of his various administrations in improving the nation's network of roads. Critics, however, claimed that in Nicaragua all roads seemed to lead to one or another Somoza family farm.

Somoza also ordered the construction of hydroelectric plants to modernize agriculture. He farsightedly sought to expand the nation's production of beef—a product for which both domestic and foreign demand was good—and to exploit the nation's gold resources.

Through skillful public relations in the United States, Somoza attracted considerable outside investment to modernize the nation's cotton plantations. Despite a surplus, the United States opened its market to Nicaraguan cotton. By the time of Tacho's death, cotton, coffee, and gold were Nicaragua's three chief exports—welcome replacements for the undependable banana exports that were vulnerable to disease.

When the elder Somoza was killed by a young Nicaraguan poet in 1956, his two sons were ready to succeed him. The older son, Luis, was president of the national congress and next in line for the presidency. The younger, Anastasio (called "Tachito" to distinguish him from his father), was chief of staff of the Guardia Nacional, control of which was essential to the Somoza dynasty.

### LUIS SOMOZA

Luis Somoza stepped in to fill his father's unexpired term in September 1956.

Educated at the University of Southern California, where he studied electrical engineering, Luis was only 35 years old when he won a full presidential term in his own right. His impressive 89 percent of the popular vote owed much to his reputation as a legislator with mildly liberal views.

As president, Luis repeatedly declared his intention to use his term of office as a "bridge to democracy." Accordingly, he liberalized the more repressive aspects of his father's administration. Critics of the Somozas were allowed greater freedom of speech. The members of Luis's cabinet exercised more authority on their own. His administration permitted trade unions to organize, even though this was a possible threat to some of the Somoza family's own business interests. Luis himself took a leading role in revising the nation's work force policy, so that it would provide protection for agricultural, as well as industrial, workers.

Luis sought to improve Nicaragua's relations with its sister republics in Central America—efforts that helped to create the Central American Common Market (CACM) in 1960. Until the CACM was thrown into disarray in 1969 following the war between El Salvador and Honduras,

Nicaragua enjoyed wider markets for its products. Average annual increases in total economic output and in personal income were impressive, and more and more Nicaraguans entered the middle class.

Cotton boosted the economy, providing needed jobs on farms, and accounted for almost half of Nicaragua's total exports. The boom in cotton provided capital to feed industrialization. The number of textile factories multiplied, as did plants for food processing, furniture making, and other light industries.

To the surprise of his compatriots, Luis Somoza requested that the Nicaraguan congress formally bar his own reelection for a second term. True to his word, he stepped down at the end of his first term, though he used the influence of his powerful family to back his own candidate in the elections of February 1963.

The candidate, René Schick Gutiérrez, a longtime employee of the Somoza regime, won an overwhelming victory in elections reported by observers on the scene to be as honest as Nicaragua had ever experienced. Luis, however, refused to allow the elections to be supervised by neutral observers from the Organization of American States—an action that caused opposition

President Tacho Somoza *(left)* raises a glass with his sons, Luis *(middle)* and Tachito.

parties to withdraw from the race. Schick, a somewhat undistinguished though widely respected man, turned in a good record as chief executive. He demonstrated some independence in his decision making, and Nicaragua showed signs of becoming more democratic. Unfortunately, however, Schick's term ended prematurely when he died of natural causes at the age of 56 in August 1966.

### TACHITO SOMOZA

The following February, Anastasio Somoza Debayle, second son of the dynasty's founder, was elected to the presidency. The outcome of the election was never in doubt, for at the time of Schick's death, Tachito was serving in the key position of chief of the armed forces.

Two months later, while Tachito was still president-elect, Luis died of a heart attack at age 45. Tachito, pledging to continue the liberalizing policies of his brother, entered office at age 41.

Tachito had been educated at the U.S. Military Academy at West Point. As chief executive, Tachito led the country into further participation in inter-American affairs. Nicaraguan troops were prominent among the members of a peacekeeping mission sent to preserve order in El Salvador and Honduras after the 100-hour war between the two nations in 1969. He also pursued law and order at home and sternly suppressed protests by students.

Like his father, Tachito tried to improve Nicaragua's agricultural production. He is credited with having introduced new varieties of rice and tobacco and new breeding stock to improve Nicaragua's growing herds of livestock—including his own.

Under Tachito's leadership, the already vast Somoza business empire expanded and in some ways began to resemble a large multinational corporation. The Somozas operated a wide variety of enterprises: ranches to raise cattle and meat-packing plants to prepare them for market, exten-

Courtesy of United Nations

**President René Schick Gutiérrez is seen arriving at the UN headquarters in New York just before his death in 1966.**

sive coffee and cotton plantations, fish-processing plants, banks, hotels, newspapers, television stations, and Nicaragua's only cement factory. They also operated the nation's only shipping line and the national airline, which boasted modern jets financed with U.S. foreign aid. General Somoza himself was the local agent for luxurious Mercedes-Benz automobiles, the preferred official vehicles.

Like his late brother, Tachito obeyed the ban against successive terms. Unlike his brother, however, he passed his power not to an elected successor but to a three-man military junta.

## The 1972 Earthquake

The military junta, which was established in May 1972, was to oversee the country until elections scheduled for 1974 could take place, but nature intervened. On December 23, 1972, a violent earthquake

struck Managua, killing 10,000 people, injuring several times that number, and destroying 50,000 homes. Downtown Managua was particularly hard hit, with 80 percent of the city's commercial establishments destroyed.

The earthquake provided Tachito with an excuse to seize the reins of power in his own name. The day after the quake, Ta- chito appointed himself president of the national emergency committee and declared martial law. This last step enabled him legally, as commander of the Guardia Nacional, to become the country's chief executive.

The general took personal charge of all relief efforts, giving orders from his personal estate, which had been spared by the

President Tachito Somoza *(middle)* holds a press conference at the United Nations in New York in 1971.

quake. He moved quickly to maintain law and order in the wake of the disaster—no small task, since most of his 6,000 officers in the Guardia Nacional had deserted their posts to look after the needs of their own earthquake-stricken families.

The global response to the disaster was quick and generous. No country's assistance was more bountiful than that of the United States, birthplace of Tachito's wife. Within hours, medical and engineering units from the U.S. Southern Command, specially trained for disaster relief, were on the ground in Managua. Tachito commissioned his son to be a captain in the Guardia Nacional and placed him in charge of handling the relief supplies.

But by then corruption was firmly entrenched at all levels of the Nicaraguan government. According to numerous reports, members of the Guardia Nacional were selling supplies provided from abroad and were demanding bribes to guard damaged properties, to obtain reconstruction permits and import licenses, and to win government contracts financed by foreign aid. Tachito and his close colleagues found many ways to get around U.S. foreign aid regulations that prohibited Nicaraguan government officials from receiving aid that would benefit them personally. As owners of the only cement plant, the Somozas reaped huge profits from the disaster, especially since Tachito's own government established building codes that required the use of cement in most rebuilding programs. The Somozas also profited from the sale of land on which a large complex of emergency housing was built.

## The Sandinista Revolution Begins

To stifle growing dissent and reports of corruption, Tachito declared that the situation following the disaster posed a threat

Downtown Managua still smoked six days after the 1972 earthquake that destroyed much of the city. The blackened area *(center)* was completely demolished.

to national security, and he imposed a state of siege in 1975. This enabled his government to suspend the constitutionally guaranteed rights of Nicaragua's citizens and to impose strict press censorship. Taking their cue from Tachito, local officers of the Guardia Nacional often took matters into their own hands, killing those suspected of anti-Somoza activities.

Human rights violations against innocent civilians brought strong criticism from officials of the Catholic Church and from international human rights guardians such as Amnesty International. In reaction to the growing repression, a revolutionary movement took form. Several groups of armed rebels took to the field, determined to overthrow the Somoza dynasty by force.

The most influential of these groups was the Sandinist National Liberation Front (FSLN), more commonly known as the Sandinistas. The FSLN—named after Augusto César Sandino, the resistance leader of the 1920s and 1930s—was founded in 1961.

Under President Jimmy Carter, the U.S. government began to put distance between itself and the Somozas. Politically moderate Nicaraguans became fearful that the excesses of the Somozas might lead to a government of the radical left. Nicaragua became a place of uneasy tensions, and people feared a civil war.

The spark that touched off the revolution occurred on January 9, 1978, when Pedro Joaquín Chamorro, the respected

Seeking to revitalize areas of downtown Managua leveled by the earthquake of 1972, the Sandinista government ordered the building of some modern, quake-resistant structures. The reconstruction of the city proceeded slowly, however, throughout the 1980s and early 1990s.

With the Somoza monopoly on the cement industry, Tachito was able to capitalize on the earthquake by establishing government building codes that required the use of cement. Here a worker stacks cement tiles in a Somoza factory.

editor of Managua's *La Prensa* newspaper, was murdered. The day after Chamorro's assassination—which was blamed on Somoza and his colleagues—30,000 people demonstrated in the streets of Managua. Buildings that housed Somoza-connected businesses were attacked and burned. From that moment on, increasingly large strikes were staged by Nicaraguan workers, who clashed violently with the Guardia Nacional.

The revolution gained momentum until, on August 22, 1978, a small force of rebels —led by Edén Pastora Gómez (called Commander Zero)—seized control of Nicaragua's National Palace, where the congress was in session. The rebels captured the legislators and several hundred officials and ransomed them for $500,000 and the release of 60 political prisoners. Somoza met the ransom demands by releasing the prisoners and granting them and the rebels safe passage into Venezuela and Panama. As the exiles proceeded to the airport, thousands of cheering Managuans lined the way to show their support for the rebels' daring act of defiance.

## The Final Sandinista Offensive

Somoza looked in vain to the United States for support, where many people were shocked by the graft, torture, and murder that had become the hallmarks of Somoza's rule. The final offensive by the now-united rebel forces consisted of coordinated attacks on the capital city from the four points of the compass and from within Managua itself. During June and July of 1979, hit-and-run firefights between rebels and Somoza forces became pitched battles from trenches. There was fighting in the streets of several cities, including Matagalpa, Estelí, and León to the north and west of Managua, and Masaya southwest of the capital.

On June 26, Brazil became the first major power in the Western Hemisphere to break relations with the Somoza government. The following day, a new U.S. ambassador arrived in Managua with instructions to secure Somoza's resignation. With ammunition running out, Somoza fled to Miami on July 17. Before leaving, in a final act of betrayal, he led his loyal Guardia Nacional to believe that the United States would send in troops to crush the rebels and install a temporary government once he was gone. The United States was not eager to have Somoza as a long-term resident, and he soon left Miami for Paraguay, where he was assassinated in 1980.

## Sandinistas in Power

The Sandinistas took over a crippled country and a divided people. From 30,000 to 50,000 Nicaraguans had been killed during the conflict. Another 100,000 had been wounded. Vengeance stalked the streets of Managua, where more than 100 Somoza followers, including many officers of the despised Guardia Nacional, were murdered.

On assuming power, the Sandinistas approved a Basic Statute that replaced the 1974 constitution and dissolved the

The fighting that led up to the revolution in 1978 and 1979 caused extensive damage, illustrated by the bombed-out block of Managua *(above)*, by the rubble surrounding the arch in León *(below left)*, and by the streets of hard-hit Estelí *(below right)*.

Photo by Latin American Service

The Guardia Nacional searches a vehicle on the highway outside of Managua after the explosion of a terrorist bomb in the capital city during the rebellion. Although the Guardia Nacional enjoyed a privileged status under the Somoza dictatorship, guard members were feared and hated by many Nicaraguans after the revolution.

courts to make way for a new system of revolutionary justice with guarantees of human rights. More than 4,000 former Guardia Nacional officers were speedily placed on trial for war crimes at people's courts with appointed judges. The majority of the guard received sentences of less than five years at trials that won praise abroad for their fairness.

## Foreign Aid

During their first year in power, the Sandinistas received foreign assistance from many quarters. Cuba supplied Nicaragua with 2,000 teachers and military advisors. The Soviet Union agreed to send technical experts to help develop the battered Nicaraguan economy. Although many members of the U.S. Congress were disturbed by this Communist support, the U.S. Congress still approved $75 million in economic aid.

Fears of a Communist takeover of the Nicaraguan revolution were heightened by the presence of Cuba's Fidel Castro at ceremonies marking the first anniversary of the Sandinista triumph. By the second anniversary, the U.S. Congress had suspended economic aid to Nicaragua because

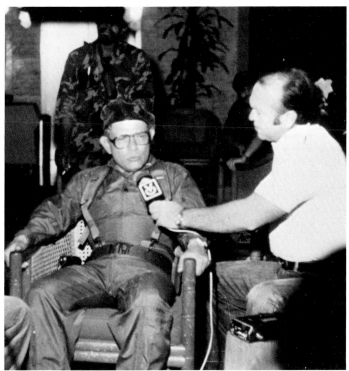

Tomás Borge Martínez, the Sandinista minister of the interior, was responsible for the country's police and security forces. Son of a drugstore owner in Matagalpa, Borge (born in 1930) was one of the oldest members of the leadership.

Photo by Latin American Service

Depicted *(from the left)* are key members of the Sandinista leadership in 1980—a year after the revolution:
- Bayardo Arce *(with beard)*, who joined the rebellion in 1969.
- Sergio Ramírez Mercado *(in civilian clothes)* became known as a leading leftist intellectual while editor of the publication *Ventana* (Window). He served as Nicaragua's vice president.
- Jaime Wheelock Román has written several books that develop Marxist thought. He served as Minister of Agrarian Reform and was one of the government's leading economists.
- Daniel Ortega Saavedra, who became politically active during student protests in the 1960s, served as president of Nicaragua.
- Dora María Tellez Agüero *(hand to her mouth)* joined the rebellion in 1973 and served as a staff officer.
- Edén Pastora Gómez led the successful seizure of the National Palace in 1978. Disillusioned by the Marxist tilt of the Sandinistas, Pastora defected in 1981 to become a leader of the contra rebellion.

Courtesy of Latin American Service

**37**

the Sandinistas were allegedly supplying arms to rebels in El Salvador. By the third anniversary in 1982, the U.S. government had released aerial photographs documenting a huge Nicaraguan military buildup that the United States portrayed as a threat to the peace of Central America. The United States and other nations also accused the Sandinistas of burning down the homes of many Miskito Indians of northern Nicaragua and driving them into refugee camps in neighboring Honduras.

## Contra Rebellion

By 1983 the Sandinistas found themselves under attack by Nicaraguans who had grown disillusioned with the revolution, including Commander Zero who had staged the daring takeover of the National Palace in 1978. With secret support from the United States, the dissenters—called contras—fielded rebel guerrilla forces. Operating from the security of bases in neighboring Costa Rica and Honduras, the contras conducted armed raids into Nicaraguan territory. It was later revealed that employees of the U.S. Central Intelligence Agency (CIA) had actually participated in one of the most devastating attacks. A predawn raid on fuel storage tanks at the Pacific port of Corinto destroyed an estimated 3.2 million gallons of

Photo by Latin American Service

In the year following the revolution, Sandinista leaders frequently addressed public gatherings to build morale and to explain their government's revolutionary goals. Sergio Ramírez Mercado has the podium, and to his right are Daniel Ortega Saavedra and Edén Pastora Gómez (seen prior to his defection from the government).

During the Sandinista regime, Nicaragua marked May Day (international Labor Day) with celebrations, marches, and speeches. The large sign to the left in the background reads, in part, "Rifle in hand, with the blood of our heroes and martyrs, the whole of Nicaragua has voted: War of Liberation, Sandinista Front."

fuel. The CIA operatives involved in the raid also mined Corinto's harbor on their way out and harbors at El Bluff and Puerto Sandino on other occasions.

In 1984 Nicaragua brought the mining before the World Court, which ruled that the United States had acted illegally. The United States, however, dismissed the ruling on the grounds that the incidents were a political matter over which the World Court had no jurisdiction. Amid escalating tensions, the Sandinistas gladly accepted military assistance from the Soviet Union —including tanks, fighter aircraft, and helicopter gunships. The United States commenced almost continuous large-scale joint maneuvers with Honduran troops near the Honduras-Nicaragua border.

## Daniel Ortega Saavedra

Bowing to international pressures, the Sandinistas held national elections, which they promised would be fair and open, on November 4, 1984. The elections, however, were viewed skeptically abroad because the major opposition parties refused to participate in them. On January 10, 1985,

Women figured prominently in the Sandinista leadership. Here Commander Dora (Dora María Tellez Agüero) addresses a rally in Managua. Dora, who came from an upper-class Conservative family, became a student activist around 1969 and later joined the rebellion while studying medicine in León at the National Autonomous University of Nicaragua.

Daniel Ortega Saavedra, who was elected Nicaragua's president in November 1984, increased ties with Soviet-bloc countries as relations with the United States became strained.

Photo by William Cameron

Photo by Latin American Service

During the 1980s, military attire was popular among the Sandinistas and their supporters. For these women, combat fatigues symbolized their advance toward equality in Nicaraguan society.

Daniel Ortega Saavedra, a Sandinista who had garnered 63 percent of the popular vote, was sworn in as Nicaragua's president at a ceremony attended by Cuba's Fidel Castro. The elections also gave the Sandinistas a two-thirds majority in the 96-member National Assembly.

In 1986 both houses of the U.S. Congress—though the margin of victory was slim in the House of Representatives—voted to continue support for the contras. Nevertheless many legislators and others in the United States feared that such extensive involvement in Central America was not warranted and might only increase the strife. The threat from the con-tras forced the Nicaraguan government to commit more than one-quarter of the national budget to defense, and President Ortega said that the contra rebellion had already cost 11,000 lives by 1986.

## Recent Events

In February 1987 Costa Rican president Oscar Arias Sánchez put forth a Central American peace proposal. Arias's plan—since referred to as the Guatemala Accord—called for scheduled cease-fires, free elections, committees to solve local disagreements, and other democratic reforms. On August 7, 1987, the chief executives of

Photo by Latin American Service

The 1981 defection of Edén Pastora Gómez, who was extremely popular among Nicaraguans, was a severe loss to the Sandinista government. Pastora later organized rebel activities in southern Nicaragua, with the support of covert assistance from the U.S. Central Intelligence Agency (CIA). On May 16, 1986, after a falling out with the CIA and with other elements of the growing rebellion, Pastora announced that he would fight no longer. Pastora sought asylum in Costa Rica, where he pledged to convert his rebel army into a political party.

Commander Dora addresses a political rally in Managua's Central Plaza.

Honduras, El Salvador, Nicaragua, Guatemala, and Costa Rica met to sign and put into effect the agreement.

To meet the terms of the Guatemala Accord, the Sandinista government announced elections for early 1990. In response, 14 conservative and liberal opposition parties united to form the National Opposition Union (UNO). This coalition threw its support to Violeta Barrios de Chamorro, the editor of *La Prensa* and the widow of Pedro Chamorro. Violeta Chamorro overcame the well-organized campaign of the Sandinistas and defeated Daniel Ortega for the presidency.

Their signing of the Guatemala Accord forced the Sandinista leaders to accept the election results, which seemed to repudiate the popular revolution of 1979. Despite their loss at the polls, many Sandinista officials remained in powerful government positions. Sandinista officials also control strong labor unions and the country's police force.

After taking office, Chamorro implemented a land reform program that was meant to redistribute land seized during the 1980s. The program ran into problems as peasants and landowners disputed their claims. In addition, Chamorro's acceptance of Sandinistas in the new government alienated many of her supporters. Chamorro broke with the UNO in January 1993. When the UNO boycotted the legislature, Sandinista representatives managed to form a new majority.

In accordance with constitutional changes passed in 1995 that bar an incumbent president from seeking re-election, Violeta Chamorro did not run in 1996. Presidential candidate for the right-wing Liberal Alliance and former mayor of Managua Arnoldo Alemán defeated former president and Sandinista candidate Daniel Ortega. Alemán is trying to bring economic stability to the country.

Nicaragua is still recovering from civil war and from the economic difficulties of the 1980s. Clashes still occur between former contras and the Sandinista-led Nicaraguan army. Although inflation has been slowed, many Nicaraguans are suffering unemployment, poverty, and hunger.

Violeta Barrios de Chamorro, president of Nicaragua from 1990 through 1996, tried to reconcile the country's competing political factions and to reform the economy.

## Governmental Structure

The Nicaraguan government is divided into three branches. The executive branch consists of the president, the vice president, and an appointed cabinet. The president is elected by popular vote for a five-year term. All adult men and women are eligible to vote.

The legislative branch of the government, the 92-member National Assembly, enacts the country's laws. The National Assembly is also elected by popular vote and has proportional representation in each of Nicaragua's 16 geographic departments. Autonomous (independent) councils govern the remote regions of the Atlantic Coast. In the Southern Atlantic Autonomous Region, the UNO party holds the most council seats, while in the Northern Atlantic region, the Miskito Indians party, YATAMA, has a majority.

The judicial branch is composed of a supreme court with appeals, district, and local courts subordinate to the supreme court. There are separate judges for labor and administrative matters.

To keep up morale and build enthusiasm for the revolution, the Sandinistas staged frequent mass rallies. When a new constitution was suspended in January 1987, however, 2,000 Managuans marched in protest without police permission.

Youngsters at a market in Managua gather at the stall of a watermelon vendor who provides music along with his wares.

# 3) The People

Nicaragua's 4.4 million people are concentrated mainly on the narrow, 10- to 40-mile-wide strip of land west of Lakes Managua and Nicaragua. Because of the migration of people from the troubled countryside to cities and villages, over half of Nicaragua's population is urban.

Like other Latin American nations, Nicaragua has a high rate of population growth, amounting to an annual increase of 3 percent. Because many adult Nicaraguans were killed in recent conflicts, Nicaragua has the youngest population of any Central American nation. Forty-four percent of Nicaragua's people are less than 15 years of age. Warfare has likewise reduced

life expectancy in Nicaragua to only 66 years.

## Mestizos, Blacks, and Indians

About 70 percent of Nicaragua's population is mestizo. Racial mixing began shortly after the arrival of the first Spanish colonists and has continued ever since.

Another 17 percent of Nicaragua's population is classified as white—people of pure Spanish blood and immigrants from other European lands. Blacks make up 9 percent of the population. They live mainly along the coasts, where the ancestors of many of them were brought to work as slaves on plantations. Other blacks, who are recent immigrants from overcrowded nations in the West Indies, have settled along the Caribbean coast.

Through intermarriage, blacks of this area have mingled their bloodlines with those of the original Indians. These native groups include the Miskitos, long settled along Nicaragua's northern Caribbean coast and along the Honduran frontier. The Sumus live mainly north of the port of Bluefields, and the Ramas live south of that city. The Miskitos came to world attention because of their forced resettlement by the Sandinistas, who reportedly burned down Miskito villages to deny refuge to anti-Sandinista rebels. In the early 1990s, many Miskitos who had fled across the border to Honduras returned to their homes in Nicaragua.

## Language and Religion

Spanish is the official language of Nicaragua and is spoken by more than 70 percent of the people. The rest speak

Courtesy of David Mangurian

Serious and hard-working, Nicaragua's people of mixed Indian-and-Spanish blood are anxious to build a better future for their children and impatient for political differences to be resolved.

Courtesy of Inter-American Development Bank

Children in a village near the Pacific coast investigate a newly installed pumping system that is now providing a reliable source of fresh drinking water. The coastal communities of Nicaragua have received much less governmental attention than cities in the interior where most of the country's population is concentrated.

During the 1980s, a billboard in Managua tracked the progress of a national campaign aimed at educating all Nicaraguans to read and write. The Sandinista regime was particularly proud of its record in promoting literacy.

English—the language of some whites, mestizos, and blacks living on the coasts— or Indian tongues that survive among about 4 percent of the people.

Most Nicaraguans are Roman Catholic and, despite the Sandinistas' attempts to downplay the role of the Church, are very devout. Churches are well attended, and the views of Catholic officials—many of them as critical of the Sandinistas as they were of the Somozas—are widely respected. Along the coasts, many blacks belong to Protestant denominations, including a number of fundamentalist (strict) congregations that have attracted a number of converts in recent years.

## Education

The Sandinista government scored a success in its national campaign to promote literacy. The government enlisted some 60,000 students to live with poor families, where the students taught the basics of

Girls enter the cathedral in Managua. Although the cathedral is now closed owing to severe damage from the 1972 earthquake, there are plans to restore it. In the early 1990s, a new cathedral built of stronger materials began rising twenty miles south of Managua. Donations from the United States and from Nicaraguans have helped pay for the cathedral's planning and construction.

46

Independent Picture Service

At the National University of Nicaragua, the basic sciences are stressed to prepare students for jobs in the development of their country.

reading and writing to family members. Nicaraguan government figures indicate that 87 percent of all Nicaraguans are now literate, compared to only 50 percent at the end of the Somoza dynasty. Moreover, government figures indicate that primary-school attendance rose steadily after the fall of the Somoza government.

School attendance is now required for children from seven to twelve years of age, although only about 70 percent of primary-age students actually attend classes. Secondary schools instruct students for another five years, starting at age 13. Many students end their studies before reaching the age of 18. There are technical and vocational schools that offer job and professional training, as well as four universities. The National University of Nicaragua has 7,000 students at campuses in Leon and Managua. The Central American University is a Roman Catholic institution in Managua.

Photo by David Mangurian

These secondary school students attend Managua's Business Institute, where they are preparing for careers as future entrepreneurs. The private sector is growing in Nicaragua, where many state-owned firms have been sold by the Chamorro government.

Under the Sandinistas, the media praised revolutionary goals and programs from socialist countries. Even the walls of buildings became billboards for revolutionary murals. This mural covered a science building at the National University in León.

## Health

During the 1980s, health care improved in Nicaragua. The Sandinista regime built new public clinics in cities as well as rural areas and funded social welfare programs. The number of doctors, nurses, and hospitals also increased.

Nevertheless, the people of Nicaragua continued to suffer from tropical diseases, such as malaria, and from poor diet, unhealthy sanitary conditions, and the violence brought by the continuing civil conflicts. Typhoid and polio remained serious threats, especially for young people in rural areas, where clinics and doctors are rare. By the mid-1990s, Nicaragua's life expectancy, 66 years, was among the lowest in Central America. Infant mortality—the number of babies who die within a year of their birth—stood at 49 per 1,000, a high rate.

In order to improve Nicaragua's economy, the Chamorro government has cut government spending on health and social services. In the early 1990s, many public clinics closed. Others now charge patients directly for their services, and as a result many people must forego treatment. New, private health facilities, however, are available to those who can afford them.

## Styles of Life

The capital city of Managua is a bustling place, where government officials and businesspeople seem to enjoy an energetic lifestyle. Restaurants, most of which serve heavily North Americanized fare, are places for wheeling and dealing. In contrast, Nicaragua's secondary cities, such as León and Granada, have a relaxed atmosphere. The style of life is more typically Latin American, with people eating a hearty lunch of rice and beans and a meat dish before taking a siesta (rest) and beginning anew the day's work.

There are sharp differences between the lives of urban and rural Nicaraguans. Many of the conveniences of the city are unavailable to rural farmers. Public transportation is difficult and sometimes nonexistent. Homes in warm coastal areas are protected by roofs of thin metal or of palm leaves. On the farms there is less entertainment, and work routines are often monotonous. People seem beaten down and resigned to their lot. Women stare at passersby from doorways, their faces expressing an ability to survive all changes and expect nothing in return.

The worst living conditions in Nicaragua prevail along both coasts among poor blacks, who live in cultural isolation from the mainstream of Nicaraguan society. By law their children are educated in Spanish, which they do not speak at home or use on the streets of port communities. Few blacks have risen to prominence on the na-

Photo by David Mangurian

Rice and beans have long been important staples in the Nicaraguan diet. The lifting of price controls, however, has made these foods more expensive.

Courtesy of Inter-American Development Bank

The family that lives in this home in the lowlands raises bananas, corn, and beans to survive. In rural areas many Nicaraguans still get by on subsistence farming.

Courtesy of Inter-American Development Bank

Animals and people share a simple life in rural Nicaragua. Though they may be poor, Nicaraguans are a proud people and determined to make progress.

tional scene, although some pursue careers as lawyers and doctors within their own English-speaking communities. The Sandinistas did little to ease conditions among poor blacks or to promote progress within black communities. No black person figured in the top ranks of the Sandinista leadership.

## Festivals and Sports

For mestizos and other Spanish-descended Nicaraguans, the year is dotted with Church-related festivals. Many religious festivals honor familiar saints. The patron saint of Managua, St. Dominic, is revered during the first 10 days of August. The St. Dominic festival is a time of religious ceremonies, spectator sports—including horse racing, bullfights (during which the bulls are not killed), and cockfights—and much colorful pageantry. Parades and processions are common during the festival.

Baseball remains the national game of preference among Nicaraguans, despite

Courtesy of David Mangurian

Many blacks along the coasts of Nicaragua live in poverty. Their plight has been ignored by national governments right down to the present time.

A festival is in progress at Diriamba, in the heart of the coffee-growing region of southwestern Nicaragua.

the Sandinista regime's efforts to dampen popular interest in U.S. major-league teams. Young people in the cities also play basketball as well as soccer. Nicaraguans, like other Central Americans, have become increasingly fond of public parks and recreational facilities. They enjoy camping among their country's beautiful mountains and near the volcanoes. In time, earthquake-devastated areas of downtown Managua may become green parks and recreational fields.

Basketball is a popular sport in Nicaragua, as is baseball, which survived the Sandinistas' censoring of the publication of U.S. major league scores.

## Fine Arts

Nicaraguan musical tastes favor contemporary popular sounds, including the rhythms of the Caribbean. In recent years more groups have begun to play music from the Third World, as the Sandinistas encourage popular identification with the struggles for liberation of oppressed peoples in other lands.

In reshaping the country's ideology, the Sandinistas do not have to compete with an illustrious cultural heritage. The exception is Rubén Darío (1867–1916), whose birthplace was renamed to honor his memory and who is honored as much today by Sandinistas as he was by previous governments. Darío (the pseudonym of Felix Rubén García Sarmiento) spent many of his 49 years living outside the homeland he celebrated in his verse. A diplomat, Darío was a strong nationalist who wrote movingly of his resentment for the U.S. Marines' occupation of Nicaragua during the last 20 years of his life.

As a stylist Darío is credited with having revolutionized Latin American literature by writing in the informal language and by experimenting with unconventional literary forms. His influence radiated throughout the Spanish-speaking world, and he is credited with having added new vitality to Spanish poetry.

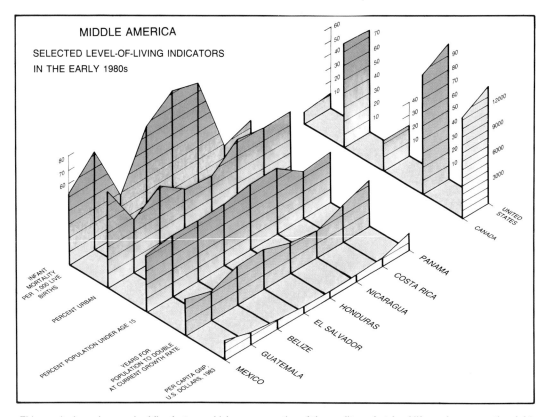

This graph shows how each of five factors, which are suggestive of the quality and style of life, varies among the eight Middle American countries. Canada and the United States are included for comparison. Data from "1986 World Population Data Sheet" (Washington, D.C.: Population Reference Bureau, Inc., 1986).

Ernesto Cardenal Martínez, Nicaragua's minister of culture, is credited with having stimulated primitive painting while working as a Catholic priest in Solentiname, a group of 38 islands in Lake Nicaragua. He encouraged local residents of the islands to establish an artists' center. This work, by islander Milagros Chavarria, is entitled *Picking Cacao*. Like other Nicaraguan painters of the primitive style, Chavarria uses beautiful, luminous colors to depict everyday activities in the lives of local people.

This monument honors Rubén Darío. The following of muses, cherubs, and swans befits Nicaragua's most outstanding poet and man of letters.

53

Courtesy of Inter-American Development Bank

The family of Alcides Ferrofino Flores proudly shows off one of the calves purchased with a government loan. Five full-grown steers owned by the family were stolen during the period leading up to the revolution. Their farm is located in the province of Chinandega, bordering Honduras.

# 4) The Economy

After taking power, Nicaragua's Sandinista leaders completely restructured the country's economy. The new government took over banks, mines, and manufacturing concerns, organizing them into about 400 state-controlled companies. The Sandinistas broke up the Somoza family estates and awarded cropland and farms to their allies in the countryside.

Throughout the 1980s, the Sandinista government received support from the Soviet Union, Cuba, and other socialist countries. Nicaragua continued to borrow, however, and Soviet assistance was not enough to meet the heavy burden of debt. As private businesses disappeared, many entrepreneurs and skilled professionals fled the country. Nicaragua's industries suffered greatly from the loss of investment capital and experienced managers.

Nicaragua suffered a gradual loss of its earning power, which was felt particularly in the cities. Shortages of goods and food—even of bread—increased. Such shortages, though caused mostly by lower production and less efficient distribution of goods, were worsened by the influx of people to the cities. Whereas only one-third of all Nicaraguans lived in the cities in 1950, that proportion had risen to three-fourths by 1994.

Emigration increased, as did grumbling among the dwindling ranks of the middle class, who were hard hit by Sandinista price controls that made what people wanted to buy expensive and what they had to sell cheap. Price controls made private business less attractive to middle-class Nicaraguans, in whom the spirit of entrepreneurship is strong.

The Sandinista government built silos for storing grain in key areas of Nicaragua to help distribute food crops efficiently. To some extent the system duplicates one that Mexico set up about 30 years ago.

This Managuan dairy plant, La Perfecta, received a loan from the Inter-American Development Bank to resume production following the 1979 revolution.

Managua's textile factories produce fabric and clothing for domestic use. The Nicarao Taxtile Plant in Managua was taken over by the Sandinista government in the 1980s. The plant became an affiliate of the national Industrial Corporation of the People, but was closed in the early 1990s.

Warfare between Sandinista forces and the Contras further damaged Nicaragua's fragile economy. Production declined in nearly all sectors, and, despite support from the Soviet bloc, the nation went further into debt. Prices rose rapidly as the Nicaraguan currency lost most of its value. When the Chamorro government took power in 1990, inflation in the country was running at several thousand percent per year.

The new government has cut its spending and has issued a new currency, the cordoba oro. As a result of these measures, inflation slowed by the mid-1990s. Nevertheless, the unemployment rate of about 23 percent has hurt urban laborers as well as returning exiles, many of whom cannot find work. Although the amount of foreign aid from Europe and the United States has increased, Nicaragua still has great difficulty in attracting new investment from abroad.

## Manufacturing

Under the Sandinista regime, industries producing half the nation's goods and services suddenly came under state ownership and control. A weakened private sector could not compete against firms that were operated and financed by the ruling

55

Members of an agricultural cooperative weed onions by hand to save money that might otherwise be spent on herbicides. The tractor in the distance, which is owned by the cooperative, is plowing a field to prepare for corn planting.

party. Although the government made a few productive investments, the country's trade did not improve. For example, Nicaragua produced sugar at more than double the world price and was able to profit only by selling sugar at artificially high prices to the Soviet Union and other socialist countries.

Nicaragua's industries also suffered extensive damage during the fighting of the 1980s. Manufacturing firms lacked the money needed to make repairs, to upgrade their machinery, and to buy raw materials. Throughout the decade, industrial production steadily declined, and most large, state-owned concerns lost money.

The Chamorro government has begun the process of selling or transferring state industries to private owners. Yet much machinery has fallen into disrepair, and many Nicaraguan products have become obsolete on the world market. The country desperately needs new foreign invest-

The spirit of small business is still strong on the streets of Managua, where vendors offer a variety of consumer goods. Note the street sign honoring General Somoza above the display of goods.

Courtesy of Inter-American Development Bank

This powdered milk plant at Matagalpa, a town northwest of Managua, was built with funding from the Inter-American Development Bank—a Western Hemisphere agency that has provided Nicaragua with much-needed capital for a wide variety of development projects.

ment to upgrade its manufacturing base and to provide jobs to its workers.

Food products, beverages, chemicals, and petroleum are the largest manufacturing sectors in Nicaragua. Most industrial output is still concentrated in Managua, where small factories process sugar, meat, cooking oil, and cocoa. Plants in Leon make leather goods, textiles, and cigars, while coffee and sugar are important products in Grenada. In 1990 manufacturing provided 16 percent of Nicaragua's goods and employed 11 percent of the work force.

## Agriculture

Before 1979 much of Nicaragua's productive land was under the control of the Somoza family. The Sandinistas broke up this monopoly and reorganized farmers on state-owned estates and cooperatives. The regime made little investment in improving farm equipment, however, and as a result harvests declined. Low prices for their crops forced many farmers off the land and into the cities. In addition, an

Courtesy of Inter-American Development Bank

In rural Nicaragua, the coffee harvest is still carried to market on mules. Little investment has been made to modernize agriculture.

inefficient distribution system led to shortages of food.

Landownership again became an important issue in the 1990s, as the new government reversed the Sandinista redistribution of land. Some farmland under Sandinista control is now being turned over to the people who worked on the estates. Other land is being rewarded to contra fighters. But poor harvests continue as a result of land disputes and the violence that continues in many rural districts.

Like other Latin American governments, Nicaragua is seeking to make life in rural areas more attractive, in order to decrease the flow of unskilled people to the cities. Increased agricultural production would also help the country's foreign trade. The government has built roads into sparsely settled areas, particularly in the eastern half of the country. Nicaraguan leaders are also working hard to resolve the conflicting claims on rural estates, many of which were seized by the Sandinistas and turned over to their loyal supporters. Despite these efforts, many rural people are still arriving in the cities in search of employment and better living conditions.

This privately owned shoe repair shop in Masaya thrived despite government controls during the 1980s.

About 10 percent of Nicaragua's land is under cultivation. In the Pacific coast region, volcanic ash has fertilized the soil and made it the most productive in the country. Nicaragua grows coffee in the Central Highlands and cotton in the Pacific region. Farmers also raise sugarcane, bananas, corn, and beans. Rice is the most important food crop. Cattle are raised for domestic consumption and for export to foreign markets. With machinery and fuel in short supply, many Nicaraguans still use horses for plowing and mules for transporting goods to market.

## Energy and Mining

During the 1980s, petroleum was imported from the Soviet Union at low prices, but the fall of the Soviet Communist government in 1991 ended this trade. Nicaragua now must import oil at higher, market prices from other suppliers. The nation's major fuel remains wood, which meets half of all energy demands. In the future, Nicaragua may be able to exploit oil and natural gas deposits off the Pacific and Caribbean coasts.

Cattle are rounded up by cowboys in rural Nicaragua.

58

Courtesy of Inter-American Development Bank

A worker packs toilet paper at a privately owned enterprise in Granada.

Nicaragua operates two geothermal plants—which use heated, underground water sources to generate power—and hydroelectric plants at Asturias and Malacatoya. The rapid streams of the Central Highlands have hydroelectric potential but will require large investments. With the help of foreign loans, Nicaragua is planning to revamp its electric power system. Engineers will repair dams, upgrade power lines, and extend electrical service to poor neighborhoods in Managua.

The conflicts of the 1980s severely hurt Nicaragua's mining industry, which depends on foreign trade. The trade embargo imposed by the United States, for example, stopped exports of copper to Germany. Lacking new investment and labor, several mines closed or cut back production. Although Nicaragua still mines small reserves of copper, gold, silver, and salt, this sector contributes less than 1 percent of the country's total production.

## Foreign Trade

The United States was Nicaragua's major trading partner before the 1979 revolution. During the 1980s, this trade ended under sanctions imposed by the U. S. govern-

ment, and Nicaragua lost its most important export market. In 1985, the first year of the trade embargo, the value of Nicaragua's exports was less than half of what it had been in the last year of Somoza's dictatorship.

The U.S. embargo cut Nicaragua off from suppliers of 80 percent of its imports, including such essentials as machinery, vehicles and spare parts, paper and paper products, and petroleum. Nicaragua also lost trade with U.S. allies such as Japan and West Germany. Japan had become an important Nicaraguan customer, buying substantial quantities of cotton. West Germany had been buying copper, cotton, and coffee in Nicaragua.

The Sandinista government accumulated a foreign debt of $5.3 billion by 1986. This was more than three times the debt left by Somoza only seven years earlier. Half of the new debts had gone to pay for essential imports to keep the Nicaraguan economy running. Little had gone to buy capital goods that might increase the country's productive capacity. In the mid-1980s, the country was paying only small amounts for imports of machinery

Courtesy of Inter-American Development Bank

A farmhand collects eggs on a chicken farm near Ciudad Darío. The farm is owned and operated by two sisters, Mercedes and Miriam Avedaño Rugama. During the revolution Sandinista guerrillas took over the farm for one month and ate 1,600 of the farm's 3,000 chickens. Following the revolution the sisters received a government loan to purchase 3,000 hens from Guatemala.

This street scene in Masaya shows a typical middle-class neighborhood in which people are suffering from shortages of goods and jobs.

Farm machinery is still in short supply in many areas of Nicaragua. These people cultivate fields the old-fashioned way, using a horse to pull a plow held by a worker walking behind.

and equipment to enlarge its industrial base.

In the early 1990s, the country also had a large trade deficit, meaning that the value of its imports exceeded that of its exports. Although the United States has lifted its trade embargo, Nicaragua still depends on agricultural staples, such as rice, coffee, and sugar, for most of its trade. As a result, farmers and other producers are vulnerable to changes in market prices for basic foods.

Coffee, meat, and cotton remain the most important exports. Nicaragua also sells bananas, sugar, and seafood abroad. The largest customers for Nicaraguan goods are Japan, the United States, Guatemala, Costa Rica, and the European Community (EC), an association of European countries. Heavy machinery, transport equipment, raw materials, fuel, and consumer goods are purchased from the United States, Mexico, and the EC.

## Transportation

A system of surfaced roads links most cities and towns of western and central Nicaragua, but the lowlands of the east remain isolated and poorly served by the nation's transportation system. The only road into eastern Nicaragua ends at the town of Rama. A boat service along the Escondido River links Rama to Bluefields.

For transport, many Nicaraguans use a public bus service. The buses link larger towns, such as Managua, Leon, and Chinandega. Crowded and inexpensive buses operate in the capital. In remote villages that have no roads, inhabitants use mules and oxcarts to travel and to transport their harvests.

The Pan-American Highway, which travels the length of Central and South America, joins several major Nicaraguan cities in the heavily populated western region. The highway skirts the shore of Lake Nicaragua before crossing the border into Costa Rica.

Nicaragua has 186 miles of railway. The major line—which links Managua, Leon, and the port of Corinto on the Pacific coast—ends at Granada. Aeronica, the national airline, runs both domestic and international flights from the Managua airport.

Courtesy of Inter-American Development Bank

Following the 1979 revolution these workers established a furniture-making cooperative that produced chairs, desks, tables, and office furniture in Managua.

Courtesy of Inter-American Develoment Bank

The Sandinistas were fortunate to be able to take over a flourishing network of credit cooperatives. Enlightened business leaders had established a nonprofit institution for the credit cooperatives several years before the Sandinista takeover.

Private enterprise continued to exist in Nicaragua under the Sandinistas. This shoemaker worked at a privately owned business in Masaya.

## The Future

Severely damaged by many years of civil war and government mismanagement, the Nicaraguan economy will take a long time to recover. The country must still make payments on its foreign debt, but this steady flow of money out of Nicaragua makes new investment in equipment and factories difficult. The Alemán government is continuing Chamorro's policy of privatizing factories and industries, but it still faces resistance from labor leaders who

Much of Nicaragua's light industrial manufacturing, which is concentrated in Managua, requires hand labor. At this candy plant, lollipops are individually wrapped.

With loans from such international financing agencies as the World Bank and the Inter-American Development Bank, Nicaragua has built hundreds of miles of new roads.

fear unemployment and cuts in social spending. In order to proceed with its plans, the government is trying to gain the cooperation of the country's powerful labor unions. The new government is also attempting to jump-start the economy by doing what the Chamorro administration was unable to do—by returning the land seized by Sandinistas to the rightful owners.

Despite losing the elections of 1990 and 1996, the Sandinistas remain an important political force. The group controls most of the land that the government is trying to redistribute. Nicaraguans worry that Alemán will follow the same path as the Chamorro government and try to cut a deal with the Sandinistas to avoid violence. Alemán's new government faces a police force and armed forces that still have many Sandinistas within their ranks. The administration must try to win the cooperation of these two groups, which

have been accused of conspiring against the government.

Former Sandinista officials still hold important offices and block efforts at the redistribution of property and land. The rift between those who support the Sandinistas and those who support the new democratic government shows no sign of being mended. Without cooperation between these two groups, Alemán's efforts to attract foreign investment and to grow the Nicaraguan economy will be fruitless. In addition, bands of contras and Sandinista-led army units have returned to remote areas to resume the battles of the 1980s.

Nicaragua desperately needs foreign investment, which would provide money for upgrading industry and for modernizing agriculture. But to attract this investment, the country must stop the continuing violence and seek ways to heal deep and bitter divisions.

**63**

# Index

To Owen & Kei –
K.G.

For Lori and Claire
E.B.

Text copyright © 2021 by Ken Geist
Illustrations copyright © 2021 by Eric Barclay

Printed in China 38 • First edition, April 2021 • Book design by Rae Crawford

There Was a
# Silly Unicorn
## Who Wanted to Fly

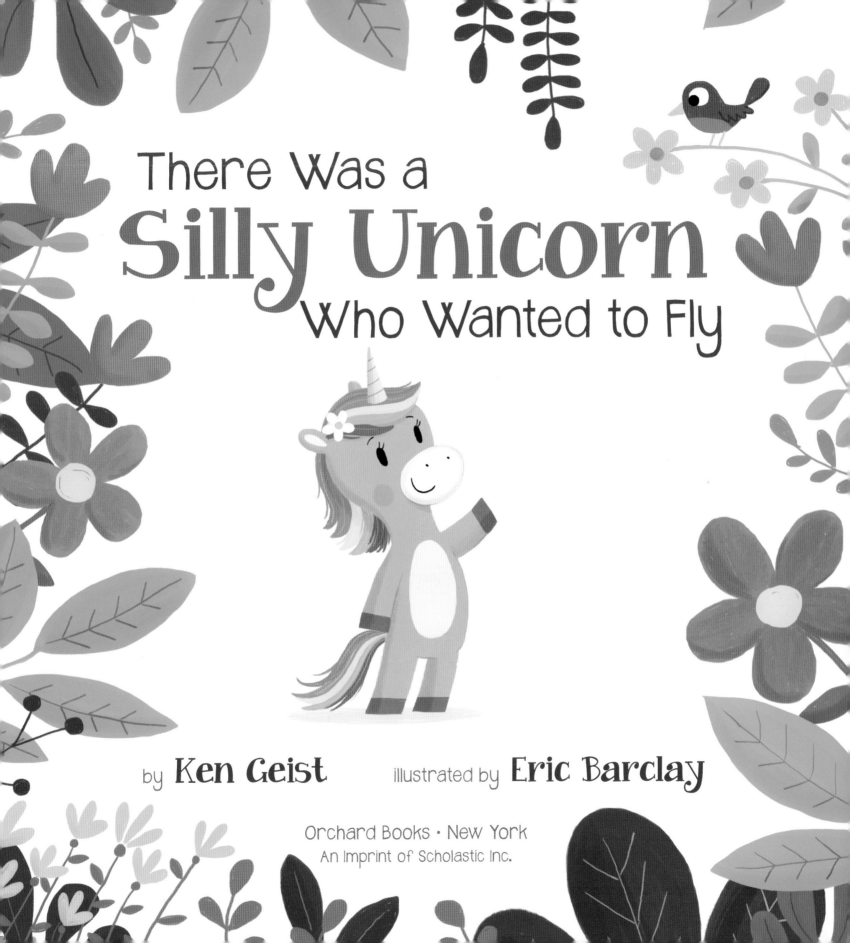

by **Ken Geist**     illustrated by **Eric Barclay**

Orchard Books · New York
An Imprint of Scholastic Inc.

There was a silly unicorn who wanted to fly.
I don't know why, but she wanted to fly.

You can't catch me!

So she gave it a try.

There was a silly unicorn who wanted to fly.
She tried by swallowing a bee, OH MY!
The buzzing would surely make her go high.

Buzz!

Buzz!

Buzz!

Buzz!

There was a silly unicorn who wanted to fly.
A flapping butterfly was the thing to try.

She swallowed
the butterfly
to help the bee,

To flutter
and buzz
and dance
with the trees.

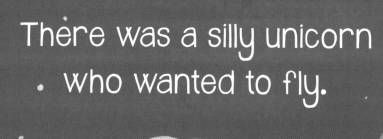

There was a silly unicorn
who wanted to fly.

Hey,
that's how
I sleep!

In swooped a bat,
she gulped with a sigh.

She swallowed the bat to help the butterfly,
Together they could float
and touch the sky.

She swallowed the owl to help the bat,
All together they flapped and flapped.

There was a silly unicorn who wanted to fly.
She caught an eagle soaring by.

She swallowed the eagle to glide with the owl,
She swallowed the owl to wing with the bat,
She swallowed the bat to flap with the butterfly,
She swallowed the butterfly to buzz with the bee,

This unicorn was silly as silly can be!

There was a silly unicorn who wanted to fly.
She saw a rainbow in the bright blue sky.

Her stomach

twitched.

Her hooves
began to rise . .

Higher

and higher,

much to her **surprise!**

She smiled and giggled
as she drifted up high,
And her magical horn tooted
a wonderful cry.

And all her friends were suddenly free . . .

To swirl and whirl and dance with the trees.